EDGE
BOOKS™

Collies, Corgis, and Other

HERDING DOGS

by Tammy Gagne

CAPSTONE PRESS
a capstone imprint

Edge Books are published by Capstone Press,
1710 Roe Crest Drive, North Mankato, Minnesota 56003
www.mycapstone.com

Library of Congress Cataloging-in-Publication Data
Names: Gagne, Tammy, author.
Title: Collies, Corgis, and other herding dogs / by Tammy Gagne.
Description: North Mankato, Minnesota : Capstone Press, [2017] | Series: Dog
    encyclopedias | Audience: Ages 9-12. | Audience: Grades 4 to 6. |
    Includes bibliographical references and index. | Description based on
    print version record and CIP data provided by publisher; resource not
    viewed.
Summary: Informative text and vivid photos introduce readers to various
    herding dog breeds.
Identifiers: LCCN 2015045095 (print) | LCCN 2015043100 (ebook) |
    ISBN 978-1-5157-0301-3 (library binding) | ISBN 978-1-5157-0309-9 (ebook pdf)
Subjects: LCSH: Herding dogs—Juvenile literature. | Dog breeds—Juvenile
    literature.
Classification: LCC SF428.6 (print) | LCC SF428.6 .G34 2017 (ebook) |
    DDC 636.737—dc23
LC record available at http://lccn.loc.gov/2015045095

Editorial Credits
Alesha Halvorson, editor; Terri Poburka, designer; Kelly Garvin, media researcher;
Katy LaVigne, production specialist

Photo Credits
Corbis: Asa Lindholm/Naturbild, 21 (top), Dorling Kindersley Ltd, 21 (bottom);
Newscom/Dorling Kindersley, 15 (b), 27 (b); Shutterstock: Aleksandra Dabrowa, 19 (t),
Alena Kazlouskaya, 22 (b), ARTSILENSE, 16 (b), Best dog photo, 10 (t), Bildagentur, 8 (t),
Csanad Kiss, 24 (b), cynoclub, 6 (t), 10 (b), 11 (b), 13 (t), Daz Stock, 26 (t), Eric Isselee,
cover (left), 6 (b), 7 (b), 8 (b), 9 (b), 12 (b), 14 (b), 18 (b), 19 (b), 29 (t), GroanGarbu, 24 (t),
HelenaQueen, 23 (b), Igor Marx, backcover, 28, Jagodka, 25 (b), JP Chretien, 9 (t), Julia
Remezova, 7 (t), Kachalkkina Veromika, 16 (t), Katho Menden, 20 (t), Ksenia Raykova,
12 (t), Lee319, 11 (t), 25 (t), Lenkadan, 14 (t), Liliya Kulianionak, 23 (t), LSphotoCZ, 1,
Mikkel Bigandt, cover (top right), 4-5, 20 (b), miroslavmisiura, cover (bottom right),
Nikolai Tsvetkov, 17, Pack-Shot, 15 (t), Sanne vd Berg Fotografie, 13 (b), Scandphoto,
18 (t), Susan Schmitz, 29 (b), Svetlana Valoueva, 22 (t), wim-eye-d, 26 (b); Superstock/
Juniors/Juniors, 27 (t)

Printed and bound in the United States of America.
009676F16

Table of Contents

Driving Dogs

The American Kennel Club's (AKC) Herding Group is made up of 29 dog breeds. Herding dogs are skilled and hardworking. Herders were first developed to drive farm animals, such as sheep and cattle. The dogs worked with ranchers to move large flocks or herds from one area to another. They would run frantically, bark aggressively, and nip at the animals' heels to move them forward.

Many herding dogs have also become popular as pets. These smart dogs enjoy being useful. Whether they are competing in an organized activity or learning commands in their own backyard, they take their jobs seriously. Many breeds have a strong desire to please their owners.

Because of their high energy levels, herding dogs aren't for everyone. They can be loud and **boisterous**. Some will even try to herd small children if they have nothing else to do. Owners must provide these dogs with plenty of activity.

Herding dogs come in a wide range of sizes and coat types. From the small Corgi to the giant Old English Sheepdog, herding-dog lovers are bound to find a breed that is right for them.

FUN FACT

The AKC was formed in 1884. The club educates dog enthusiasts about 189 different dog breeds in the form of dog shows and other organized events.

Australian Cattle Dog

FUN FACT

The Australian Cattle Dog is also known as the Blue Heeler and the Red Heeler.

Appearance:

Height: 17 to 20 inches (43 to 51 centimeters)
Weight: 30 to 45 pounds (14 to 20 kilograms)

Australian Cattle Dogs have a short, double coat. It comes in either blue-gray or brown-red. Some dogs have dark fur around one or both eyes. This marking makes it look like the dog is wearing a mask.

Personality: Australian Cattle Dogs make loving and loyal pets. When they work as cattle herders, Australian Cattle Dogs are determined and courageous.

Breed Background: The breed was developed by crossing a type of Collie and a Dalmatian.

Country of Origin: Australia

Recognized by AKC: 1980

Training Notes: Australian Cattle Dogs are smart and highly trainable. They respond especially well to rewards. Some owners train Australian Cattle Dogs for performance events, such as herding or **agility** competitions.

Care Notes: Australian Cattle Dogs can make great pets for the right people. Owners should be prepared to provide plenty of activity though. The breed needs two to three hours of exercise each day.

Australian Shepherd

Appearance:
Height: 18 to 23 inches (46 to 58 cm)
Weight: 40 to 65 pounds (18 to 29 kg)

The Australian Shepherd has medium-length fur. Many Aussies are merles, which means that the coat has a mixture of dark patches and lighter markings.

Personality: Aussies have strong personalities. Bred to herd sheep, they can be pushy pets. Some have even been known to try to herd children.

Country of Origin:
United States

Recognized by AKC: 1991

Training Notes:
Australian Shepherds are highly intelligent and eager to please their owners. Positive training methods, such as treats and lots of praise, work best with this breed.

Care Notes: Although the Aussie's coat is long, this breed doesn't need a lot of grooming. Regular brushing and occasional baths are usually enough to keep this dog clean and comfortable.

FUN FACT
After World War II (1939–1945), the Aussie's popularity skyrocketed when these dogs were shown in many movies, on television, and in rodeos and horse shows.

FAMOUS DOGS
The main character of the children's book *Henry the Dog with No Tail* is an Australian Shepherd. Aussies do have tails. They are just naturally short.

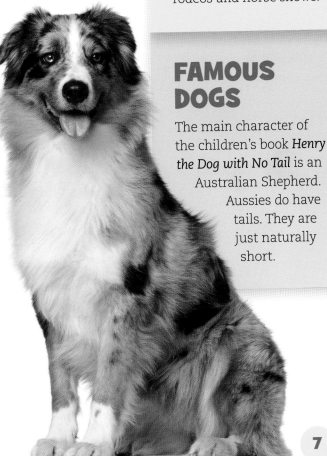

Bearded Collie

Appearance:

Height: 20 to 22 inches (51 to 56 cm)
Weight: 45 to 55 pounds (20 to 25 kg)

Bearded Collie puppies are born with a mixture of dark and white fur. As they move into adulthood, the darker color lightens. Beardies are often confused with Old English Sheepdogs. A Bearded Collie has a much longer tail, however.

Personality: Owners describe the Bearded Collie's personality as energetic. This lively breed enjoys bouncing around and playing. Beardies also love kids, but they can be a bit too rough for small children.

Country of Origin: Scotland

Recognized by AKC: 1976

Training Notes: Beardies are strong-willed dogs. They need early training with **socialization**. This means meeting new people and other animals.

Care Notes: This long-haired breed needs a fair amount of grooming. Weekly brushing keeps tangles from forming. The breed also needs a bath every six to eight weeks.

Beauceron

Appearance:
Height: 24 to 28 inches (61 to 71 cm)
Weight: 65 to 85 pounds (29 to 39 kg)

The Beauceron has a short, smooth coat. The hair is slightly longer on the dog's neck, tail, and backside. Most Beaucerons are black and tan. Some also have gray markings. These dogs are called harlequins.

Personality: This devoted breed will work hard to please its owner. Beaucerons also have a strong **instinct** to protect their families.

Breed Background: Like many herding dogs, Beaucerons were developed to drive sheep and cattle. Many Beaucerons still perform this work in Europe.

Country of Origin: France

Recognized by AKC: 2007

Training Notes: Training this intelligent breed is easy but important. Owners who don't properly train their Beaucerons can end up with a domineering pet.

Care Notes: Beaucerons are happiest when they have a purpose. These active dogs need to exercise both their bodies and their brains regularly. Organized activities, such as agility, are ideal for this breed.

FUN FACT

This dog takes more time to mature than many other breeds—three years!

Belgian Malinois

Appearance:
Height: 22 to 26 inches (56 to 66 cm)
Weight: 60 to 65 pounds (27 to 29 kg)

The Belgian Malinois (say MAL-in-wah) has a black muzzle and ears. Its main coat color is tan or brown-red. Light-colored dogs are called **fawn**. Darker Mals are called mahogany.

Personality: This breed loves its human family. It takes time to warm up to strangers, however. The Belgian Malinois does well with older children. It can also live peacefully with other pets if it is raised with them.

Breed Background: The Belgian Malinois was developed as a sheepherder. Today members of this breed are best known for their work as police and military dogs.

Country of Origin: Belgium

Recognized by AKC: 1959

Training Notes: The Belgian Malinois needs consistent training. Pups especially need socialization during their first six months of life.

Care Notes: The Mal's short coat makes grooming a simple task. These dogs do shed though. Regular brushing can help keep dead hair off carpets and furniture.

FUN FACT

The Belgian Malinois often runs in large circles. This habit comes from the breed's herding instinct.

FAMOUS DOGS

A Belgian Malinois named Cairo was part of United States Navy SEAL Team Six. He helped the SEALs find Osama Bin Laden in 2011.

Belgian Sheepdog

Appearance:
Height: 22 to 26 inches (56 to 66 cm)
Weight: 40 to 75 pounds (18 to 34 kg)

The Belgian Sheepdog has long, black hair. Some dogs have a black and white coat too. This breed's double coat is shorter on its head, ears, and lower legs.

Personality: Belgian Sheepdogs love spending time with their human family members. This breed can make a confident, devoted companion. Belgian Sheepdogs love to feel like they have a purpose or job to do.

Breed Background: The Belgian Sheepdog and the Belgian Malinois are closely related. At one time they were even considered variations of the same breed.

Country of Origin: Belgium

Recognized by AKC: 1912

Training Notes: Similar to the Belgian Malinois, the Belgian Sheepdog needs early training. These dogs are smart and quick learners. They are also commonly trained as police or military dogs or for search-and-rescue work.

Care Notes: The Belgian Sheepdog sheds year-round. It needs to be brushed weekly. A fenced yard is also important. Belgian Sheepdogs have been known to chase passing joggers or bicyclists.

FUN FACT
During World War I (1914–1918), Belgian Sheepdogs worked on the battlefields as message carriers and ambulance dogs.

Border Collie

Appearance:
Height: 18 to 23 inches (46 to 58 cm)
Weight: 30 to 45 pounds (14 to 20 kg)

Border Collies come in a variety of colors and patterns. A Border Collie can have a medium-length coat or a short, smooth coat. Common colors for Border Collies are black and white, but there are 17 total color variations.

Personality: Border Collies are best known for their intelligence and high energy. Due to their tendency to herd, Border Collies do best with older children.

FUN FACT
Underneath all that hair is a surprising amount of muscle. These dogs are natural athletes.

Breed Background: The Border Collie is named for its area of origin. This dog was developed between England and Scotland.

Country of Origin: United Kingdom

Recognized by AKC: 1995

Training Notes: If not properly trained, these dogs can become destructive and aggressive. Early socialization and crate training are important for Border Collies.

Care Notes: Border Collies need a lot of physical exercise. They also require mental **stimulation**. Canine sports, such as flyball or fetch, can help satisfy both these needs.

Bouvier des Flandres

Appearance:
Height: 23 to 37 inches (58 to 94 cm)
Weight: 60 to 90 pounds (27 to 41 kg)

The Bouvier des Flandres has a thick coat, including fawn, salt and pepper, and brindle, which is brown with streaks. The fur covers the dog's face, forming its famous mustache and beard.

Personality: Bouviers are extremely dedicated animals. They make loyal pets, but they should be supervised around children and other animals.

Breed Background: Belgian monks developed the Bouvier des Flandres breed. *Bouvier* means "cattle herder" in French.

Country of Origin: Belgium

Recognized by AKC: 1931

Training Notes: These dogs are smart but independent. Bouviers need lots of training with positive reinforcement, such as praise and treats.

Care Notes: These large, energetic dogs need plenty of room to run around. Bouviers also need to be brushed often to keep **mats** from forming.

FUN FACT
Bouviers worked as military dogs in World War I and World War II.

13

Briard

Appearance:

Height: 22 to 27 inches (56 to 69 cm)
Weight: 50 to 100 pounds (23 to 45 kg)

The Briard has long black, gray, or yellow-brown fur covering its body and face. The breed is also known for its J-shaped tail.

FUN FACT

President Thomas Jefferson brought the first Briards to the United States.

Personality: Briards make wonderful family pets. They are loyal, love kids, and want to be part of all household activities.

Country of Origin: France

Recognized by AKC: 1928

Training Notes: Briards are very independent, so owners need patience when teaching this breed commands. These dogs tend to be suspicious of strangers, so early socialization is important.

Care Notes: Briard owners must be willing to brush their dogs every other day. Tangles form quickly in this breed's long hair.

Canaan Dog

Appearance:

Height: 19 to 24 inches (48 to 61 cm)
Weight: 35 to 55 pounds (16 to 25 kg)

The Canaan Dog has a square-shaped body. The Canaan's double coat is short but protective. It keeps the animal warm in the winter and cool in the summer.

Personality: Canaans are naturally curious. They love exploring. Canaans also bond closely with their human family members.

Breed Background: Nomadic desert people in the Middle East developed this rare breed. Canaan is the ancient name for Israel.

Country of Origin: Israel

Recognized by AKC: 1997

Training Notes: This breed can be easy to train if **obedience** training and socialization begin early. Otherwise a Canaan might try to dominate its owner.

Care Notes: Canaans need plenty of space and exercise. The short coat makes this dog easy to groom. Because it is a seasonal shedder, some brushing is necessary.

FUN FACT

The Canaan Dog was the first breed used to sniff for land mines in war regions.

Cardigan Welsh Corgi

FUN FACT

The Cardigan's low height is helpful in herding. If a cow tries to kick the animal, chances are good that its hoof will go right over this dog's body!

Appearance:

Height: 10 to 13 inches (25 to 33 cm)
Weight: 25 to 38 pounds (11 to 17 kg)

The Cardigan Welsh Corgi stands low to the ground. While not tall, the Corgi is definitely long. Corgis are often called Yard Long Dogs. They measure roughly one yard (0.9 meters) from nose to tail.

Personality: The Cardigan is a small dog with a big personality. It is driven and determined. It gets along well with older kids and makes a pleasant pet. It may try to herd young children, however.

Country of Origin: Wales

Recognized by AKC: 1935

Training Notes: Cardigans are smart and easily trained. They are natural guardians, so socialization is important during early training.

Care Notes: A Corgi has more back problems than many other breeds due to its long, low back. Owners should not allow a Corgi to jump off a bed or other furniture. For exercise, a Corgi loves daily walks.

Collie

Appearance:
Height: 22 to 26 inches (56 to 66 cm)
Weight: 50 to 75 pounds (23 to 34 kg)

Collies come in a variety of colors, including sable, black and tan, and white. Many Collies have long, thick double coats. Other members of the breed have shorter, smooth coats.

Personality: Collies are known for their extreme devotion. Though independent they share a deep bond with their human family members.

Breed Background: The Collie's self-direction was considered a plus in its development. These herding dogs didn't just follow commands—they thought for themselves.

Country of Origin: Scotland

Recognized by AKC: 1885

Training Notes: Collies are intelligent and easily trained. They are good listeners too. Gentle, positive training works best with these dogs.

Care Notes: Owners should never give a Collie a common medication called ivermectin. Found in many **heartworm** pills, this drug can make this breed seriously ill. The medicine also has the same effect on Australian Shepherds, Shetland Sheepdogs, and Old English Sheepdogs. A Collie needs plenty of daily exercise. This dog's long hair should be brushed weekly.

FUN FACT

Millionaire banker J.P. Morgan bought a champion Collie in 1904. He paid $4,000 for the dog named Wishaw Clinker. Today that would be like spending $100,000 on a Collie.

Finnish Lapphund

FUN FACT

Finnish Lapphunds were first bred to be dark colored so they would stand out in the snow.

Appearance:

Height: 16 to 21 inches (41 to 53 cm)
Weight: 33 to 53 pounds (15 to 24 kg)

The Finnish Lapphund comes in many colors. The most common are black and brown. Lappies sometimes have tan or white markings. The breed's long, double coat protects it from the cold.

Personality: Many people see the Finnish Lapphund as the perfect pet. Lappies are calm and friendly with people. Their gentle **temperament** makes them great matches for families with kids.

Breed Background: The Finnish Lapphund was developed for hard work in cold temperatures, such as herding reindeer.

Country of Origin: Finland

Recognized by AKC: 2011

Training Notes: The Finnish Lapphund is eager to learn and quick to train. When properly trained, these dogs get along well with people and other animals.

Care Notes: This breed is born with a soft coat that requires a lot of grooming. As the dog gets older, the coat becomes rougher. Weekly brushings will help keep a Lappie's coat looking its best.

German Shepherd Dog

Appearance:
Height: 22 to 26 inches (56 to 66 cm)
Weight: 75 to 95 pounds (34 to 43 kg)

German Shepherd Dogs are one of the most recognizable breeds. Their coats come in a wide range of colors and patterns. Most members of the breed have a black saddle with red, silver, or tan hair on other parts of the body.

Personality: German Shepherds are loyal animals and make good family pets. They often bond most closely with just one person in the household, however.

Country of Origin: Germany

Recognized by AKC: 1908

Training Notes: The German Shepherd is considered one of the smartest dog breeds. Training this breed is easy. An untrained German Shepherd, however, can be dangerous. Its bite is stronger than nearly all other dog breeds'.

Care Notes: Grooming a German Shepherd Dog isn't difficult. The breed does shed heavily though. Regular brushing can keep loose hair off owners and their belongings.

FUN FACT

A German Shepherd trained to work as a police dog can cost up to $15,000.

FAMOUS DOGS

A German Shepherd called Rin Tin Tin appeared in silent films in the 1920s. The character would later be played by two of the original dog's **descendants** on television.

Icelandic Sheepdog

FUN FACT

Many dogs of this breed have double dewclaws. Working Icelandic Sheepdogs use these extra toes to get around on ice and snow.

Appearance:

Height: 16 to 18 inches (41 to 46 cm)
Weight: 20 to 40 pounds (9 to 18 kg)

The Icelandic Sheepdog comes in numerous colors and combinations, such as black and white, chocolate and white, and red and white. The coat length can be either long or short. This breed's bushy tail curls up over its back.

Personality: Owners describe this rare breed as happy and easygoing. Icelandic Sheepdogs make affectionate pets. They love spending time with people. Many owners also find that this breed makes an ideal therapy dog. Dogs with this important job visit hospital patients to raise their spirits.

Breed Background: Foreign breeds brought **distemper** into Iceland between the 1920s and 1960s. The disease nearly caused the Icelandic Sheepdog to become extinct.

Country of Origin: Iceland

Recognized by AKC: 2010

Training Notes: Icelandic Sheepdogs are easy to train. Because these dogs are so smart, they often excel at dog competitions and sports.

Care Notes: Caring for an Icelandic Sheepdog requires lots of brushing because it is a heavy shedder. An Icelandic Sheepdog also needs regular exercise.

Norwegian Buhund

Appearance:
Height: 16 to 18 inches (41 to 46 cm)
Weight: 26 to 40 pounds (12 to 18 kg)

The Norwegian Buhund comes in two colors: black and wheaten, which is yellow-brown. Wheaten can range from cream to bright orange. A Buhund may also have a black mask or white markings.

FUN FACT

The Norwegian Buhund's nickname is the "Friendly Spitz."

Personality: This friendly breed stands out for its strong desire to please its owners. The Norwegian Buhund loves people, including children.

Breed Background:
The Buhund is a Spitz breed. Belonging to several different AKC groups, Spitz dogs all descended from dogs in the Arctic region. A Spitz has dense fur, pointed ears, and a pointed snout.

Country of Origin: Norway

Recognized by AKC: 2009

Training Notes: The Buhund can be independent, but this dog learns quickly. Basic obedience and socialization training is also important from a young age.

Care Notes: This breed has a lot of energy. A Norwegian Buhund must run and play each day. Its coat is easy to care for, requiring occasional brushing and bathing.

Old English Sheepdog

Appearance:

Height: 20 to 24 inches (51 to 61 cm)
Weight: 60 to 90 pounds (27 to 41 kg)

The first thing anyone notices about the Old English Sheepdog is its wild, fluffy coat. Although it comes in several colors, the hair is usually gray and white.

Personality: This breed is known for its hoarse bark. Because these dogs are so big, kids may try to ride them. This isn't safe for either the child or the dog. As long as kids understand how to properly treat this friendly animal, an Old English Sheepdog can make a great family pet.

Country of Origin: England

Recognized by AKC: 1888

Training Notes: Obedience training is a must, due to the breed's large size and level of energy. But do not overwork an Old English Sheepdog. Because bone growth continues for the first year and a half of their lives, it is more prone to injury during early training.

Care Notes: Old English Sheepdogs need lots of care and attention. Owners must spend about three to four hours each week on grooming. The energetic breed also needs about two hours of exercise each day.

Pembroke Welsh Corgi

Appearance:

Height: 10 to 12 inches (25 to 30 cm)
Weight: up to 30 pounds (14 kg)

The Pembroke Welsh Corgi's body is about one and a half times as long as it is tall. It is a double-coated breed. The inner coat is short and thick with longer, coarser hair over it.

Personality: The Pembroke Welsh Corgi has a lot of confidence for such a little dog. Perhaps that is why this breed was used to herd cattle. These dogs love their family members and make great pets though.

Country of Origin: Wales

Recognized by AKC: 1934

Training Notes: This smart breed is eager to learn new things and to please its owner. Pembrokes also respond well to mental challenges, such as playing fetch.

Care Notes: Pembrokes should be kept on a sensible canine diet. This breed is prone to weight gain if owners overfeed their dogs. Exercise is also important for this lively breed.

FUN FACT

The easiest way to tell the difference between this breed and the Cardigan Welsh Corgi is looking at their tails—the Pembroke doesn't have one!

FAMOUS DOGS

Great Britain's Queen Elizabeth II has owned more than 30 Pembroke Welsh Corgis during her reign.

Puli

Appearance:

Height: 15 to 18 inches (38 to 46 cm)
Weight: 25 to 35 pounds (11 to 16 kg)

The Puli stands out in any crowd. Its corded fur makes the dog look like a giant mop. These cords protect the dog from harsh weather. Though some dogs are white or gray, most members of this breed are black.

Personality: Pulik, the plural of Puli, are highly social. They love being the center of attention. They can make good pets for people with older children. They may be too rowdy for younger kids, however.

Country of Origin: Hungary

Recognized by AKC: 1936

Training Notes: Pulik are smart and trainable. They do best when training begins early and remains consistent throughout adulthood.

Care Notes: Pulik are active animals and need daily exercise. Grooming them also takes effort and time. It can take a full day for a dog to fully dry from a bath.

FUN FACT

The Puli is a rare breed. Fewer than 150 Pulik are registered with the AKC each year. Some breeds, such as the Golden Retriever, make up 60,000 annual registrations.

Shetland Sheepdog

Appearance:
Height: 13 to 16 inches (33 to 41 cm)
Weight: about 20 pounds (9 kg)

Shetland Sheepdogs have long, double coats. They come in a variety of colors. Sable and white is one of the most popular.

Personality: Shelties have a lot of energy. They like to play and tend to bark frequently. Active families are often the best matches for these dogs. They also love to play with children.

Breed Background: The breed was developed on the Shetland Islands northeast of Scotland.

Country of Origin: Scotland

Recognized by AKC: 1911

Training Notes: Shelties are among the smartest dog breeds and are easy to train. Shelties may bark and try to herd people. Basic socialization and command training should begin early on.

Care Notes: Shelties are heavy shedders. Regular brushing is important. Brushing also helps prevents mats, which can cause skin problems in this breed.

FUN FACT

A Sheltie inspired the popular video game *Nintendogs*.

Spanish Water Dog

Appearance:

Height: 16 to 20 inches (41 to 51 cm)
Weight: 31 to 48 pounds (14 to 22 kg)

The Spanish Water Dog is covered with thick, curly hair. Its coat ranges from solid colors to various shades of black, brown, beige, or white.

Personality: Spanish Water Dogs love their human families dearly. These dogs are known for being protective. They are cautious with strangers, however. Once their owners introduce them to new people, they get along with them just fine.

Breed Background: Records of Spanish Water Dogs go back almost 1,000 years. The breed's history includes a lot more than herding. These dogs were used as **vermin** hunters and as fishermen's helpers in their native country.

Country of Origin: Spain

Recognized by AKC: 2015

Training Notes: These smart dogs learn quickly with positive training. Spanish Water Dogs enjoy feeling like they have a specific job to do, and they're eager to please their owners.

Care Notes: Spanish Water Dogs should be groomed occasionally, including brushing and bathing. These dogs also enjoy daily exercise and other outdoor activities, such as hiking.

Swedish Vallhund

Appearance:
Height: 11 to 14 inches (28 to 36 cm)
Weight: 22 to 35 pounds (10 to 16 kg)

The Swedish Vallhund's low body, short coat, and perky ears make it look like a Corgi. These dogs come in combinations of gray, red, black, blue, white, or yellow.

Personality: The Swedish Vallhund enjoys being on the go. These dogs are ideal for active people. They also have their own language called "argle bargle," which is a mix of yips, barks, and howls.

Country of Origin: Sweden

Recognized by AKC: 2007

Training Notes: Swedish Vallhunds are easy to train. It is important to keep the tone positive though. This breed does not respond well to loud voices.

Care Notes: The Swedish Vallhund needs a lot of exercise. The breed loves long walks. Owners can also take this breed along when hiking. Its short coat requires occasional brushing and bathing.

FUN FACT

The Swedish Vallhund's tail comes in a few varieties—no tail, a stub tail, or a full curl tail.

Other Herding Breeds

Belgian Tervuren

Known for: being closely related to the Belgian Sheepdog
Country of Origin: Belgium
Recognized by AKC: 1959

....

Bergamasco

Known for: having a corded coat
Country of Origin: Italy
Recognized by AKC: 2015

....

Berger Picard

Known for: being the dog from the movie *Because of Winn-Dixie*
Country of Origin: France
Recognized by AKC: 2015

....

Entlebucher Mountain Dog ▶

Known for: being the smallest of the four Swiss Mountain Dogs
Country of Origin: Switzerland
Recognized by AKC: 2001

Miniature American Shepherd

Known for: being a smaller version of the Australian Shepherd
Country of Origin: United States
Recognized by AKC: 2015

....

Polish Lowland Sheepdog ▶

Known for: fearlessly protecting their flocks from predators
Country of Origin: Poland
Recognized by AKC: 2001

....

Pyrenean Shepherd ▶

Known for: living in the Pyrenees Mountains for centuries
Country of Origin: France and Spain
Recognized by AKC: 2009

....

Glossary

agility (uh-GI-luh-tee)—the ability to move fast and easily

boisterous (BOI-stur-uhss)—noisy, energetic, and rowdy

descendant (di-SEN-duhnt)—a person or animal who comes from a particular group of ancestors

distemper (diss-TEMP-uhr)—an often deadly disease common among dogs that is caused by a virus; symptoms of distemper include fever and loss of appetite

fawn (FAWN)—a light brown color

gait (GATE)—a way of walking

heartworm (HART-wurm)—a tiny worm carried by mosquitoes that enters a dog's heart and slowly destroys it

instinct (IN-stingkt)—behavior that is natural rather than learned

mat (MAT)—a thick, tangled mass of hair

obedience (oh-BEE-dee-uhns)—obeying rules and commands

socialize (SOH-shuh-lize)—to train to get along with people and other dogs

stimulate (STIM-yuh-late)—to encourage interest or activity in a person or animal

temperament (TEM-pur-uh-muhnt)—the combination of an animal's behavior and personality; the way an animal usually acts or responds to situations shows its temperament

vermin (VUR-min)—any of various small, common insects or animals that are harmful pests

Read More

Guillain, Charlotte. *Dogs*. Animal Abilities. Chicago: Raintree, 2013.

Krämer, Eva-Maria. *Get to Know Dog Breeds: The 200 Most Popular Breeds*. Get to Know Cat, Dog, and Horse Breeds. Berkeley Heights, N.J.: Enslow Publishers, 2014.

Rustad, Martha E.H. *Dogs*. Little Scientist. North Mankato, Minn.: Capstone Press, 2015.

Internet Sites

FactHound offers a safe, fun way to find Internet sites related to this book. All of the sites on FactHound have been researched by our staff.

Here's all you do:

Visit *www.facthound.com*

Type in this code: 9781515703013

Check out projects, games and lots more at
www.capstonekids.com

Index